Writer´s Workbook

A Personal Planner with Tips, Checklists and Guidelines

by Tanja Hanika

The "Writer´s Workbook" is meant as a notebook of ideas for authors who are in the process of plotting a novel. It contains help with the key phases of the writing experience, from character development and plot structure to creating marketing plans for your novel.

There are clear guidelines, checklists and planning structures for you to use throughout this guide, as well as helpful information on plot devices, such as choosing a narrative style and writing a plot synopsis.

Author Tanja Hanika has drawn on her lengthy writing experiences, and the lessons she learnt during her studies of literature at the University of Treves, to create the "Writer´s Workbook", which aims to support the process of writing for authors.

Project Title: _____

_____

_____

Start Date: _____

End Date: _____

2nd edition, October 2019
All rights reserved.
© Tanja Hanika, 2017
Original title: »Arbeitsbuch für Schriftsteller«

www.tanja-hanika.de
kontakt@tanja-hanika.de
Gartenstr. 12, 54595 Weinsheim, Germany

Using:
© Jag_cz / Fotolia.com
© FontGrube AH / Fontriver.com
© OpenClipartVectors / pixabay.com
© ClkerFreeVectorImages / pixabay.com
© Pixaline / pixabay.com
© geralt / pixabay.com
© Jjuni / pixabay.com
© QYOU / pixabay.com

Translation edited by Amy Durant and Victoria Griffin.

Please get in touch with your comments and feedback via my email: kontakt@tanja-hanika.de.
I look forward to hearing from you, and will consider your thoughts for the next edition.

Contents

Groundwork: Elaboration of the Basic Concept

Mindmaps for Initial Ideas ... 5

Brainstorming: Title, Cover, Pitch, Blurb ... 6

Premise ... 7

Setting and Point of View ... 8

Genre ... 10

Research ... 11

Building Tension ... 12

Plot Development Through Goal, Motivation and Conflict ... 13

Conflict ... 14

Character Development

Character Abstract ... 15

Four Types of Main Character ... 16

Character Types ... 17

Character Profiles ... 18

Protagonist: Background Story and Key Moments Including Impact ... 36

Antagonist: Background Story and Key Moments Including Impact ... 37

Casting - Which Qualities do the Protagonist and the Antagonist need? ... 38

Protagonist vs. Antagonist – Stages of the Conflict ... 39

Plotdevelopment and Plotstructure

The Protagonist´s Journey ... 40

Dan Wells´ Seven Point Story Structure ... 42

Michael Hauge´s Six Stages of Plot ... 43

Gustav Freytag´s Pyramid of Drama ... 44

Chekhov´s Gun ... 45

Timeline ... 46

Locations ... 48

The First Sentence and the First Chapter ... 49

The Arc Between First and Last Chapter ... 51

The End of the Novel: Crisis, Climax and Solution ... 52

Writer´s Workbook © Tanja Hanika, www.tanja-hanika.de

Finishing Work

Marketing

Mindmaps for Initial Ideas

Use these maps to write down and arrange your initial ideas on characters, plot, important themes and key scenes ...

Brainstorming: Title, Cover, Pitch, Blurb

Ideas for the Title:

-
-
-
-
-
-
-

Ideas for the Cover:

\#

\#

\#

\#

Pitch Draft:

_____

_____

_____

_____

_____

_____

_____

_____

_____

_____

Blurb Draft:

Premise

A premise is the basic message of the story. In the course of the story, the premise will be elaborated on. It shows the key motivations and conflicts for the protagonist, and what will happen as a result of these.

➡

➡

➡

➡

_____

_____

_____

_____

_____

_____

_____

_____

_____

_____

_____

Premise:

Setting and Point of View

Where is the novel set?:

When is the novel set? And over what time period?:

Point of View:

[   ] <u>Personal Narrator</u>: [   ] Third-Person,   [   ] You-   or [   ] First-Person Narrator

[   ] subjective   or   [   ] objective

[   ] <u>Omniscient Narrator</u>   [   ] <u>Neutral Narrator</u>

[   ] Present   [   ] Past   [   ] Future

                                      © Tanja Hanika, www.tanja-hanika.de

Personal Narrator:
Usually told in the first-person, this narrates the story from the perspective of the author. This is normally used for memoirs, and to narrate a true story.

Third-Person Narrator:
This gives an objective view, without narrating the story from any one character's perspective. It does not give an insight into personal thoughts or feelings, and so makes the narrative more neutral.

Second-Person Narrator:
This is a rare narrative form in which a narrator addresses the reader directly and reports on 'your' experiences.

First-Person Narrator:
This narrates the story from the point of view of one of the character's in the novel (usually the protagonist). This point of view is restricted because only the own thoughts and feelings of the narrator can be described authentically.

Omniscient Narrator:
This narrator knows everything about the characters, their feelings and the plot. He leads the reader through the action, and decides when he/she gets to know plot details. This narrator can talk directly to the reader.

Neutral Narrator:
This is neither the point of view of a character nor of a narrator. A kind of objective, invisible observer tells the story.

Setting:
The story's place and time.

Genre

Genre of my novel: _____

_____

Which guidelines do I want to adhere to?

> _____

> _____

> _____

> _____

> _____

> _____

> _____

> _____

Which conventions do I want to break?

> _____

> _____

> _____

> _____

> _____

> _____

> _____

> _____

Research

Most important resources:

Most important results:

-
-
-
-
-
-
-

To be pursued:

■

■

■

■

Building Tension

> Tension develops when the author withholds knowledge from the reader. The reader tends to gain understanding as the protagonist does.

Which core issue should occupy the reader?

Plot Development Through Goal, Motivation and Conflict

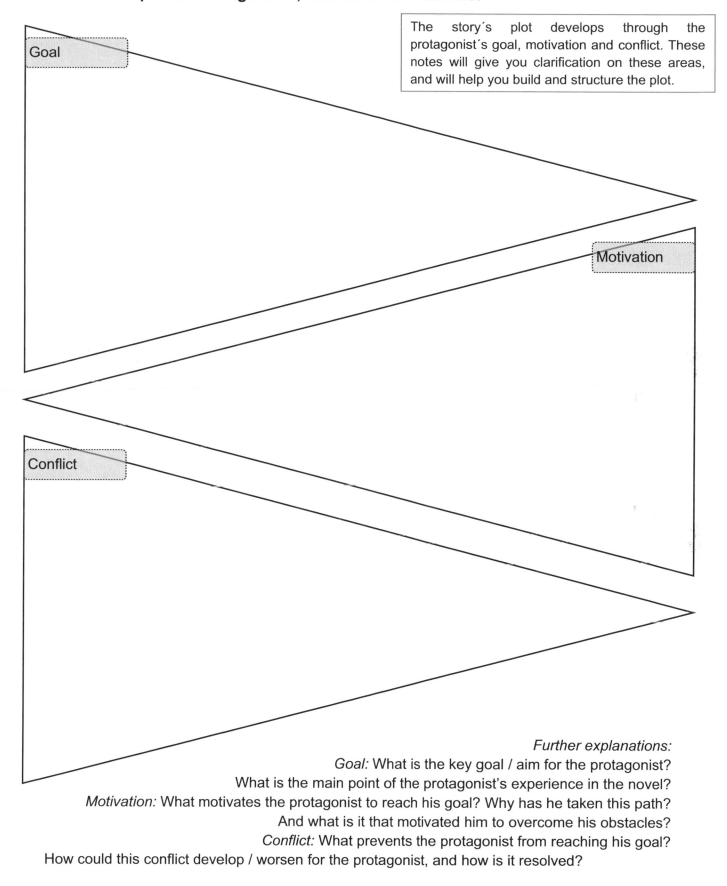

Goal

Motivation

Conflict

The story's plot develops through the protagonist's goal, motivation and conflict. These notes will give you clarification on these areas, and will help you build and structure the plot.

Further explanations:
Goal: What is the key goal / aim for the protagonist?
What is the main point of the protagonist's experience in the novel?
Motivation: What motivates the protagonist to reach his goal? Why has he taken this path?
And what is it that motivated him to overcome his obstacles?
Conflict: What prevents the protagonist from reaching his goal?
How could this conflict develop / worsen for the protagonist, and how is it resolved?

Conflict

A simplified abstract of the conflict at different stages of the narrative for the protagonist, and how the conflict is resolved.

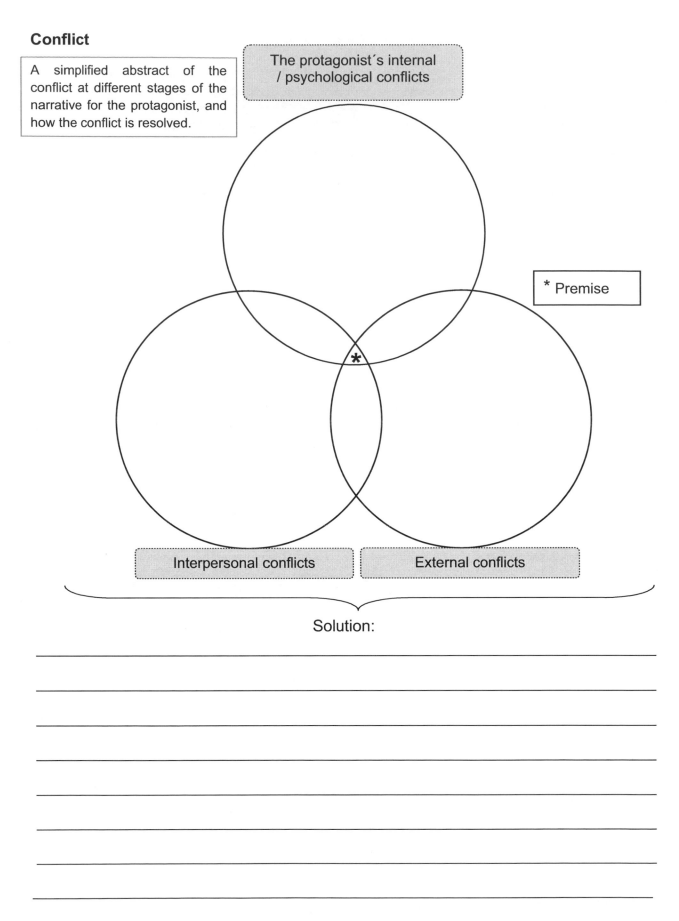

The protagonist´s internal / psychological conflicts

* Premise

Interpersonal conflicts

External conflicts

Solution:

_____

_____

_____

_____

_____

_____

_____

_____

Character Abstract

What is the function of each character, and what are their most important details/ characteristics.

Name	Function	Important Details

_____

_____

_____

_____

_____

Four Types of Main Character

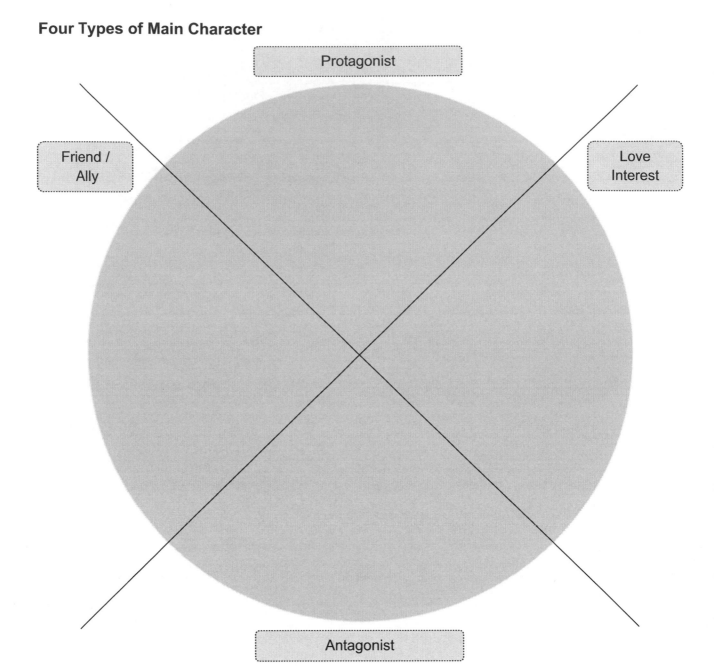

Further explanations:
Protagonist: The protagonist is the main character in the story, who determines the action and develops through the novel.
Antagonist: He or she is the protagonist´s opponent. The antagonist provides the main challenge for the protagonist in the narrative.
Friend / Ally: He or she supports the protagonist at important stages of the story.
Love Interest: He or she is the character who the protagonist wishes to become romantically involved with.

Character Types

Dynamic Characters

Static Characters

Mirror Characters

Contrast Characters

Further explanations:

Dynamic Characters: These characters hold main roles in the action of the plot, and develop throughout the narrative.

Static Characters: Side characters serve a purpose for a short part of the narrative to advance the events of the plot. The reader does not need many details about them.

Mirror Characters: These characters mirror certain motivations of characteristics of the protagonist, to illuminate important details.

Contrast Characters: These show oppositions between the protagonist and the antagonist, for instance about their motivations or their personalities.

Character Profiles

Name: _____

Function in the text: _____

Main desires: _____

_____

Age, height, weight: _____

Appearance: _____

_____

Job: _____

History: _____

_____

_____

Social background: _____

_____

Hobbies: _____

_____

Sexuality: _____

Religion: _____

Specifics: _____

_____

Good characteristics: _____

Bad characteristics: _____

Inner conflicts: _____

_____

Goals: _____

Weaknesses: _____

Development: _____

_____

Family: _____

_____

Friends: _____

_____

Enemies: _____

_____

Language: _____

_____

Habits: _____

_____

Introduction into the text: _____

_____

_____

_____

_____

_____

_____

_____

Name: _____

Function in the text: _____

Main desires: _____

_____

Age, height, weight: _____

Appearance: _____

_____

Job: _____

History: _____

_____

_____

Social background: _____

_____

Hobbies: _____

_____

Sexuality: _____

Religion: _____

Specifics: _____

_____

Good characteristics: _____

Bad characteristics: _____

Inner conflicts: _____

_____

Goals: _____

Weaknesses: _____

Development: _____

_____

Family: _____

_____

Friends: _____

_____

Enemies: _____

_____

Language: _____

_____

Habits: _____

_____

Introduction into the text: _____

_____

_____

_____

_____

_____

_____

_____

Name: _____

Function in the text: _____

Main desires: _____

_____

Age, height, weight: _____

Appearance: _____

_____

Job: _____

History: _____

_____

_____

Social background: _____

_____

Hobbies: _____

_____

Sexuality: _____

Religion: _____

Specifics: _____

_____

Good characteristics: _____

Bad characteristics: _____

Inner conflicts: _____

_____

Goals: _____

Weaknesses: _____

Development: _____

_____

Family: _____

_____

Friends: _____

_____

Enemies: _____

_____

Language: _____

_____

Habits: _____

_____

Introduction into the text: _____

_____

_____

_____

_____

_____

_____

Name: _____

Function in the text: _____

Main desires: _____

_____

Age, height, weight: _____

Appearance: _____

_____

Job: _____

History: _____

_____

_____

Social background: _____

_____

Hobbies: _____

_____

Sexuality: _____

Religion: _____

Specifics: _____

_____

Good characteristics: _____

Bad characteristics: _____

Inner conflicts: _____

_____

Goals: _____

Weaknesses: _____

Development: _____

_____

Family: _____

_____

Friends: _____

_____

Enemies: _____

_____

Language: _____

_____

Habits: _____

_____

Introduction into the text: _____

_____

_____

_____

_____

_____

_____

_____

Name: _____

Function in the text: _____

Main desires: _____

_____

Age, height, weight: _____

Appearance: _____

_____

Job: _____

History: _____

_____

_____

Social background: _____

_____

Hobbies: _____

_____

Sexuality: _____

Religion: _____

Specifics: _____

_____

Good characteristics: _____

Bad characteristics: _____

Inner conflicts: _____

_____

Goals: _____

Weaknesses: _____

Development: _____

_____

Family: _____

_____

Friends: _____

_____

Enemies: _____

_____

Language: _____

_____

Habits: _____

_____

Introduction into the text: _____

_____

_____

_____

_____

_____

_____

_____

Name: _____

Function in the text: _____

Main desires: _____

_____

Age, height, weight: _____

Appearance: _____

_____

Job: _____

History: _____

_____

_____

Social background: _____

_____

Hobbies: _____

_____

Sexuality: _____

Religion: _____

Specifics: _____

_____

Good characteristics: _____

Bad characteristics: _____

Inner conflicts: _____

_____

Goals: _____

Weaknesses: _____

Development: _____

_____

Family: _____

_____

Friends: _____

_____

Enemies: _____

_____

Language: _____

_____

Habits: _____

_____

Introduction into the text: _____

_____

_____

_____

_____

_____

_____

_____

Name: _____

Function in the text: _____

Main desires: _____

_____

Age, height, weight: _____

Appearance: _____

_____

Job: _____

History: _____

_____

_____

Social background: _____

_____

Hobbies: _____

_____

Sexuality: _____

Religion: _____

Specifics: _____

_____

Good characteristics: _____

Bad characteristics: _____

Inner conflicts: _____

_____

Goals: _____

Weaknesses: _____

Development: _____

_____

Family: _____

_____

Friends: _____

_____

Enemies: _____

_____

Language: _____

_____

Habits: _____

_____

Introduction into the text: _____

_____

_____

_____

_____

_____

_____

_____

Name: _____

Function in the text: _____

Main desires: _____

_____

Age, height, weight: _____

Appearance: _____

_____

Job: _____

History: _____

_____

_____

Social background: _____

_____

Hobbies: _____

_____

Sexuality: _____

Religion: _____

Specifics: _____

_____

Good characteristics: _____

Bad characteristics: _____

Inner conflicts: _____

_____

Goals: _____

Weaknesses: _____

Development: _____

_____

Family: _____

_____

Friends: _____

_____

Enemies: _____

_____

Language: _____

_____

Habits: _____

_____

Introduction into the text: _____

_____

_____

_____

_____

_____

_____

_____

Name: _____

Function in the text: _____

Main desires: _____

_____

Age, height, weight: _____

Appearance: _____

_____

Job: _____

History: _____

_____

_____

Social background: _____

_____

Hobbies: _____

_____

Sexuality: _____

Religion: _____

Specifics: _____

_____

Good characteristics: _____

Bad characteristics: _____

Inner conflicts: _____

_____

Goals: _____

Weaknesses: _____

Development: _____

_____

Family: _____

_____

Friends: _____

_____

Enemies: _____

_____

Language: _____

_____

Habits: _____

_____

Introduction into the text: _____

_____

_____

_____

_____

_____

_____

_____

Protagonist: Background Story and Key Moments Including Impact

The background story forms the character before the story starts, and will influence the character's motivations and goal. This will normally be integrated throughout the narrative.

It is better to weave aspects of the character's past into the plot fluidly, rather than including a lot of flashbacks to develop him and the narrative. Above all you should remember: *show, don't tell!*

Background Story / Key Moment: 　　　　　　　*Impact on Behaviour:*

＞

Background Story / Key Moment: 　　　　　　　*Impact on Fears:*

＞

Background Story / Key Moment: 　　　　　　　*Impact on Weaknesses & Assets:*

＞

Background Story / Key Moment: 　　　　　　　*Impact on Aims:*

＞

Antagonist: Background Story and Key Moments Including Impact

The background story forms the character before the story starts, and will influence the character's motivations and goal. This will normally be integrated throughout the narrative.
It is better to weave aspects of the character's past into the plot fluidly, rather than including a lot of flashbacks to develop him and the narrative. Above all you should remember: *show, don't tell!*

Background Story / Key Moment:

_____

_____

_____

_____

Impact on Behaviour:

_____

_____

_____

_____

Background Story / Key Moment:

_____

_____

_____

_____

Impact on Fears:

_____

_____

_____

_____

Background Story / Key Moment:

_____

_____

_____

_____

Impact on Weaknesses & Assets:

_____

_____

_____

_____

Background Story / Key Moment:

_____

_____

_____

_____

Impact on Aims:

_____

_____

_____

_____

Casting - Which Qualities do the Protagonist and the Antagonist need?

Protagonist   *Antagonist*

Main Goal

Plans to make the other one fail

Strengths and Weaknesses

Characteristics that surprise the reader

Where do they seem to fail?

Most important characteristics:

Protagonist vs. Antagonist – Stages of the Conflict

1.

2.

3.

4.

5.

6.

7.

8.

9.

10.

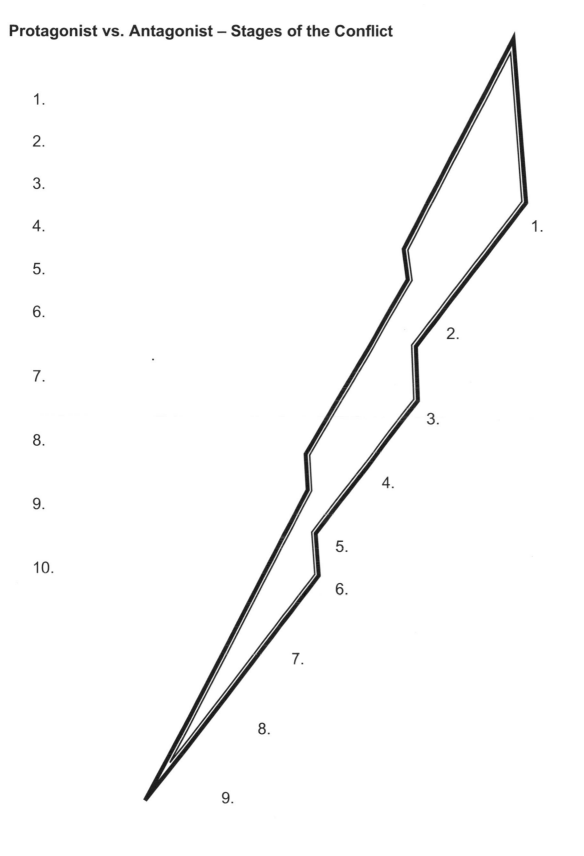

1.

2.

3.

4.

5.

6.

7.

8.

9.

10.

The Hero´s Journey

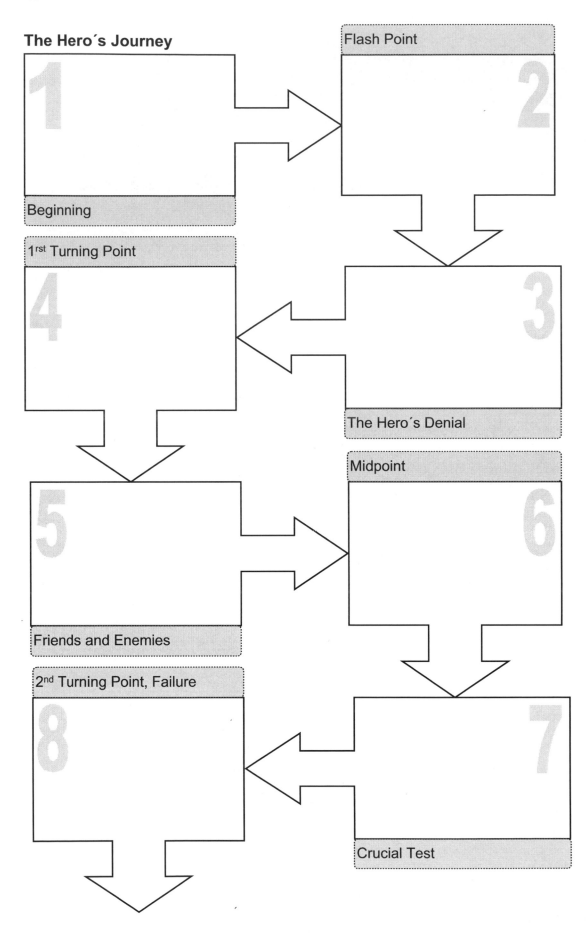

1 — Beginning

2 — Flash Point

3 — The Hero´s Denial

4 — 1rst Turning Point

5 — Friends and Enemies

6 — Midpoint

7 — Crucial Test

8 — 2nd Turning Point, Failure

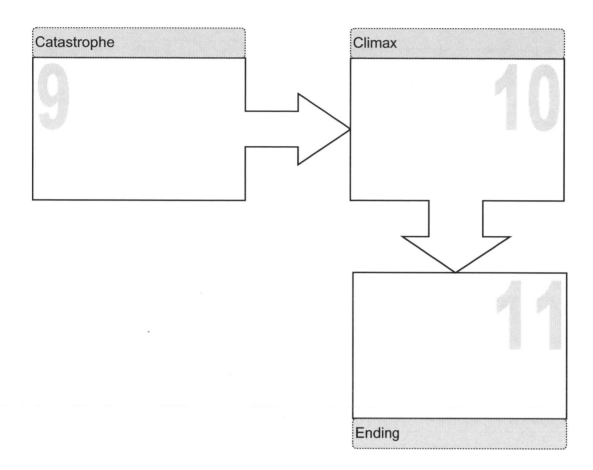

Further explanations:

1. Beginning: Protagonist has a problem, which he believes he cannot solve.

2. Flash Point: This incident pulls the protagonist out of his daily life. He has to react.

3. The Hero´s Denial: Anxiety or weakness causes the protagonist to refuse the mission at first.

4. First Turning Point: The protagonist realizes his strength and gets active.

5. Friends and Enemies: Encounter with friends, allies, enemies and problems.

6. Midpoint: The protagonist fights for his goal.

7. Crucial Test: The protagonist´s goal and inner desires come into conflict.

8. Second Turning Point, Failure: The protagonist fails in achieving his goal, his desires, or both.

9. Catastrophe: The protagonist suffers.

10. Climax: The protagonist achieves his goal at last.

11. Ending: Everything is resolved. The protagonist is fully developed.

Dan Wells´ Seven Point Story Structure

Hook (Point of departure in opposition to the solution at the end)

Plot Turn 1 (Inciting incident)

Pinch 1 (Situation sharpens, and the protagonist has to act)

Midpoint (Protagonist is fully involved in the story)

Pinch 2 (Situation sharpens again and seems hopeless)

Plot Turn 2 (Turning point, protagonist realizes how to achieve his aim)

Resolution (Conflict is positively or negatively solved for the protagonist)

Michael Hauges Six Stages of Plot

Hauge developed this structure at first for screenplays, but his concept of using six phases and five turning points can be used for every narrative story.

Act 1	Phase 1: Beginning	0%
	Phase 2: Change	10%
Act 2	Phase 3: Progress	25%
	Phase 4: Complications and Impediments	50%
Act 3	Phase 5: Final Push	75%
	Phase 6: Aftermath	90%
		100%

Possibility

Changing Plans

Point Of No Return

Biggest Regression

Climax

Gustav Freytags Pyramid of Drama

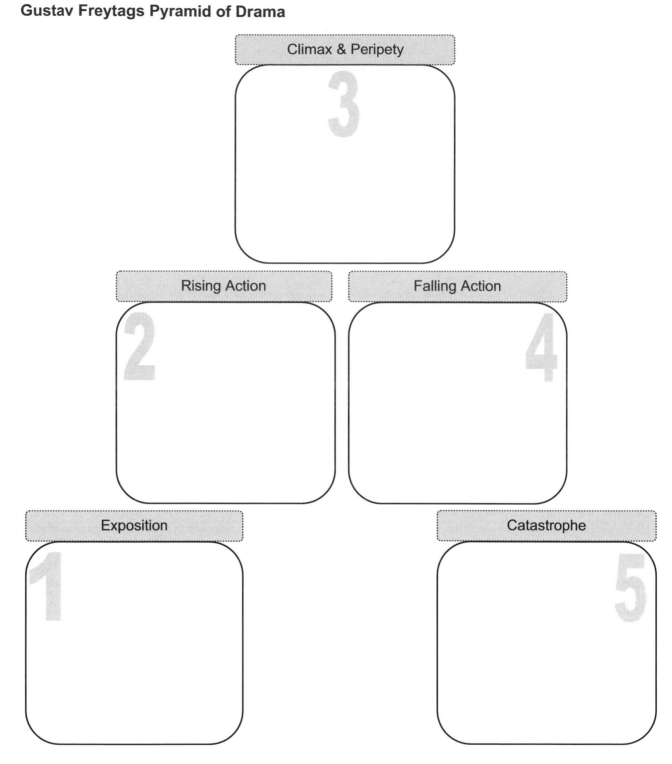

Exposition: Introduction of location and time, history, most important characters and main conflict.
Rising Action: Inciting incident, entanglement of story strands, building tension.
Climax & Peripety: Climax of tension, which leads to victory or defeat of the protagonist.
Falling Action: Action nears its end with a last increase of tension, victory or defeat is doubtful.
Catastrophe: Solution of the conflict: protagonist's ruin in the tragedy, victory in the comedy (including exhilarant storyline before!)

Chekhov´s Gun

Special details can be planned here, which shall be picked up later on.

Every piece of information, every detail, object, setting or main action that is used in the story needs to fulfill a purpose later on.

Detail	Purpose

Timeline

For chapters, scenes, stages of the protagonist´s development and notes.

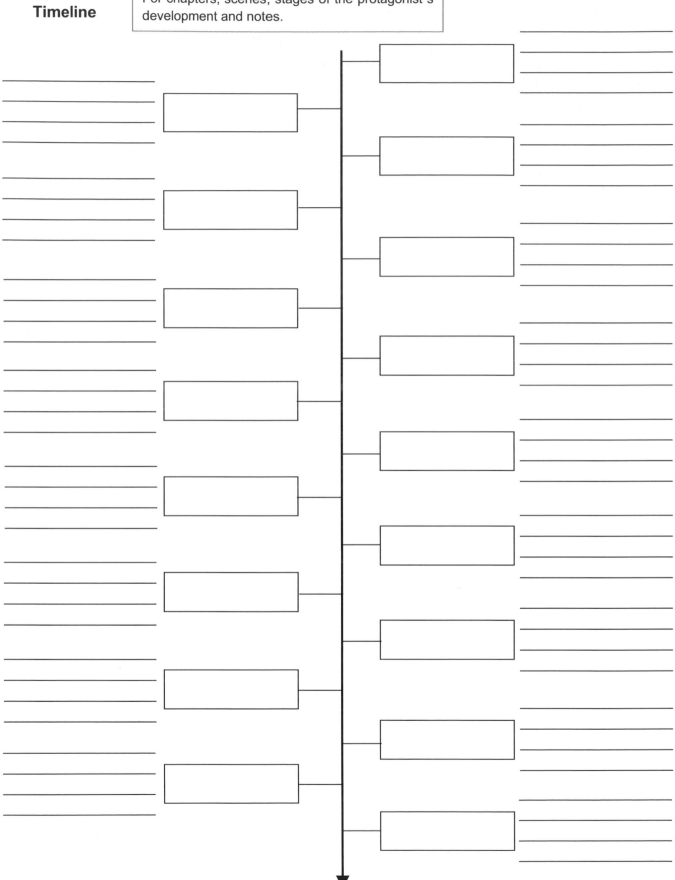

Locations

Geographical Location:

Description:

Special Characteristics:

Geographical Location:

Description:

Special Characteristics:

Geographical Location:

Description:

Special Characteristics:

Geographical Location:

Description:

Special Characteristics:

The First Sentence and the First Chapter

> The beginning of the novel is very important. You need to hold the reader's interested so they read on.

In the opening pages the rules are set: the author sets a promise for the reader, letting him or her know what kind of story he or she can expect.

1. Protagonist:
What about the protagonist is interesting enough to warrant a whole novel?

_____

_____

_____

_____

2. Narrative Voice:
Who tells the story? Why? What is special about the narrative voice?

_____

_____

_____

_____

3. Setting / World: [see Locations p. 45]
o Even if not everything will be included in the book make sure you know enough detail about the setting (history, politics, language, geography etc.).
o Is there too much information? Do I give only the facts necessary for understanding the plot.
o Do I give enough information for the reader to be able to understand everything?
o Does everything adhere to physical laws? Or have you created a new world with different physical laws? If so, are they consistent?

4. Major Problem: [see Premise p. 7]

_____

_____

_____

_____

5. The Right Moment to Begin:
Should you have started the story later on for a higher level of suspense?

_____

_____

_____

_____

The First Sentence:

_____

_____

_____

_____

_____

_____

_____

Summary of the first pages / of the first chapter:

_____

_____

_____

_____

Key plot points in the following pages:

> _____

> _____

> _____

> _____

> _____

> _____

> _____

The Arc Between the First and Last Chapter

This can also be used for other sections / stations in the text. For example, use an arrow to connect the beginning to the ending, or from part 3 to 6 and so on.

Important points
in the first chapter:

How to these points are resolved
in the last chapter:

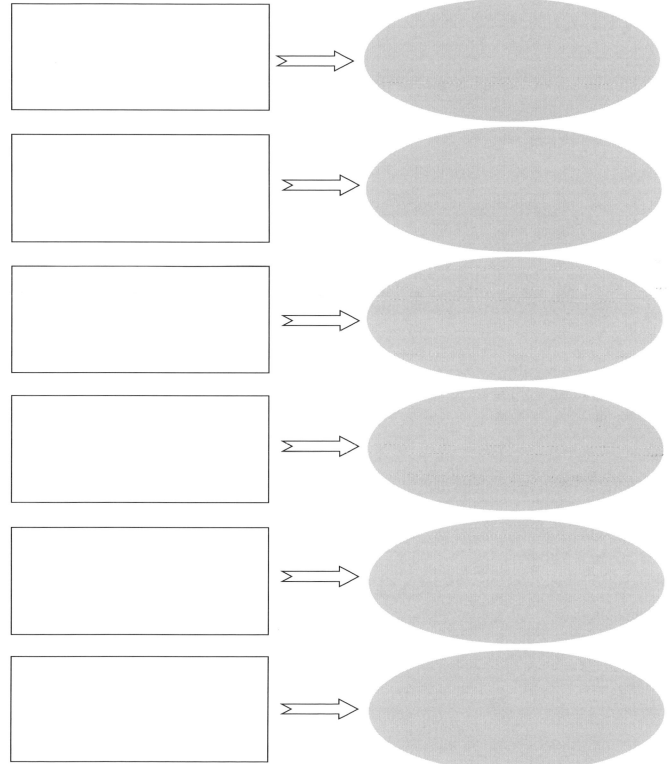

The End of the Novel: Crisis, Climax and Solution

A bad ending can spoil the whole story. The reader does not want to be on his or her own, but wants to see the strands be brought together. All relevant questions should be answered. Together, crisis, climax and solution should resolve the narrative.

Crisis (Rising tension towards the end)

Climax (Main conflict reaches peak)

Solution (Denouement: conflict solved, impact on the protagonist)

List of Open Questions

(see: Building Tension p. 12)

Which questions should occupy the reader? When and how should they be resolved?

Question:	
Point in Narrative / Chapter of Solution:	
For the Reader:	For the Character ( ):

Question:	
Point in Narrative / Chapter of Solution:	
For the Reader:	For the Character ( ):

Question:	
Point in Narrative / Chapter of Solution:	
For the Reader:	For the Character ( ):

Question:	
Point in Narrative / Chapter of Solution:	
For the Reader:	For the Character ( ):

Question:	
Point in Narrative / Chapter of Solution:	
For the Reader:	For the Character ( ):

Question:	
Point in Narrative / Chapter of Solution:	
For the Reader:	For the Character ( ):

Question:	
Point in Narrative / Chapter of Solution:	
For the Reader:	For the Character ( ):

Question:

Point in Narrative / Chapter of Solution:

For the Reader:	For the Character ( ):

Question:

Point in Narrative / Chapter of Solution:

For the Reader:	For the Character ( ):

Question:

Point in Narrative / Chapter of Solution:

For the Reader:	For the Character ( ):

Question:

Point in Narrative / Chapter of Solution:

For the Reader:	For the Character ( ):

Question:

Point in Narrative / Chapter of Solution:

For the Reader:	For the Character ( ):

Question:

Point in Narrative / Chapter of Solution:

For the Reader:	For the Character ( ):

Question:

Point in Narrative / Chapter of Solution:

For the Reader:	For the Character ( ):

Emotions – Scenes with outstanding emotional Relevance

> To focus on a small but important detail in the scene often raises more emotions than describing the whole picture.

What should the reader feel?	Plotpoints in the Scene?	Most important Detail?

Main Plot and Subplot

Double Plot:
Main story strand and side story strands stand side by side.

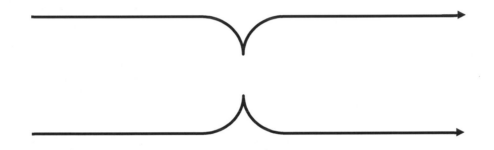

Hourglass-Plot:
Two main story strands, which run parallel to each other, collide in the middle of the novel and separate thereafter. Each stands on its own, as well as connecting to the other.

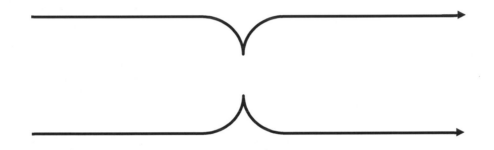

Picaresque Plot:
A series of episodic adventures, usually told from the point of view of a 'roguish', but likeable protagonist.

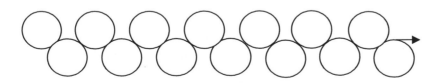

Plan for the Plot

_____

_____

_____

_____

_____

_____

_____

_____

_____

_____

_____

_____

_____

_____

_____

_____

_____

_____

_____

_____

_____

_____

_____

Chapter Summary

Chapter	Characters Involved	Plot

Chapter	Characters Involved	Plot

Brainstorming: A Title for each Chapter

Chapter	Possible Title

Personal Checklist for the First Completed Draft

Page/Chapter	What Needs Changing	

Checklist for the First Draft

Editing Issues: Plot	
Is the premise interesting enough?	
Do the setting and story fit together?	
Is the plot of the whole story, and of each individual chapter logical?	
Does the arc of tension work?	
Is the recurrent theme obvious?	
Are the intersections of the chapters elaborated on?	
Are there enough conflicts in the text?	
Are there twists in the story?	
Are enough open questions interspersed?	
Are they answered or at least picked up later on?	
Are the guidelines of the genre hold / broken as planned?	
Editing Issues: Characters	
Is there at least one character the reader can identify with?	
Are the characters deep enough?	
Do the protagonists have strong goals?	
Do the antagonists have strong goals?	
Do the protagonists develop throughout the narrative?	
Do the characters stay true to their personalities?	
Have you removed any stereotypes and clichés?	
Editing Issues: Language	
Is the chosen point of view consistent throughout?	
Is the pace of narration fitting and varied?	
Were lengthy passages deleted?	
Were short passages broadened?	
Is there the right amount of description?	
Are the dialogues authentic and fluent?	
Is the language as active as possible?	
Are the comparisons and metaphors coherent?	
Are the filler words eliminated?	
Are repetitions removed and corrected?	
Are adjectives and adverbs used sparingly?	
Are participles used sparingly?	
Other Issues to Address	

Blurb

General Points:

- × Beside the cover and the title, the blurb is the most important marketing device for a novel. This is what will capture the reader's interest.
- × The blurb should not contain any false or misleading information so that the product will satisfy the consumer´s expectations.
- × The reader should be able to identify the genre of the book by reading the blurb.
- × The blurb should not reveal too much information! At this point, the reader does not want to know what happens at the first turning point.
- × There should not be any grammatical or orthographical mistakes in the blub.
- × Is there anything that makes the book unique? Point it out.

Formalities:

- × Use short, comprehensible sentences.
- × The blurb should be written in third person singular, in the past tense.
- × The blurb should be short and contain between 100 and 150 words.
- × Do not end it with a question, if possible.

Content:

- × Introduce the protagonist and the most important characters and at least indicate the antagonist.
- × Describe the setting. Where and when does the story take place?
- × Mention the catalyst, the main hindrance and which consequences threaten the protagonist.
- × Imply that there will be a twist.

(See first Draft p. 6)

Checklist:

Protagonist: _____

Setting (where and when?): _____

Catalyst of the Plot: _____

Antagonist: _____

Main Hindrance: _____

Consequences: _____

Indication of the Twist: _____

_____

_____

_____

_____

_____

_____

_____

_____

_____

_____

_____

_____

Title and Cover

Title, cover and blurb should fit the content of the book. Most important is to gain the reader's attention. Current trends can inspire which book they choose to read.

Title Ideas:

1. _____

2. _____

3. _____

Tip:
Check if your title is free to be used.

Cover Drafts:

Dedication, Acknowledgement and Postface

Draft of the dedication:

Who should be mentioned in the dcknowledgement?
-
-
-
-
-
-
-
-

Notes for the postface:

■

■

■

■

■

■

■

■

■

■

Key Documents and Changes Made

Document Title	What was changed?

Example:

Project title - first draft.docx	Raw version of the text
Project title - corr1.docx	Character development, plot aim reached?
Project title - corr 2.docx	Arcs of suspense? Chapter transitions, dialogues, show don´t tell
Project title - corr 3.docx	Language
Project title - corr ….docx	…
Project title - corr betas.docx	Editing on the basis of beta reader´s comments
Project title - corr lec.docx	Including the editorial report
Project title - final.docx	Final version of the book

Marketing Ideas

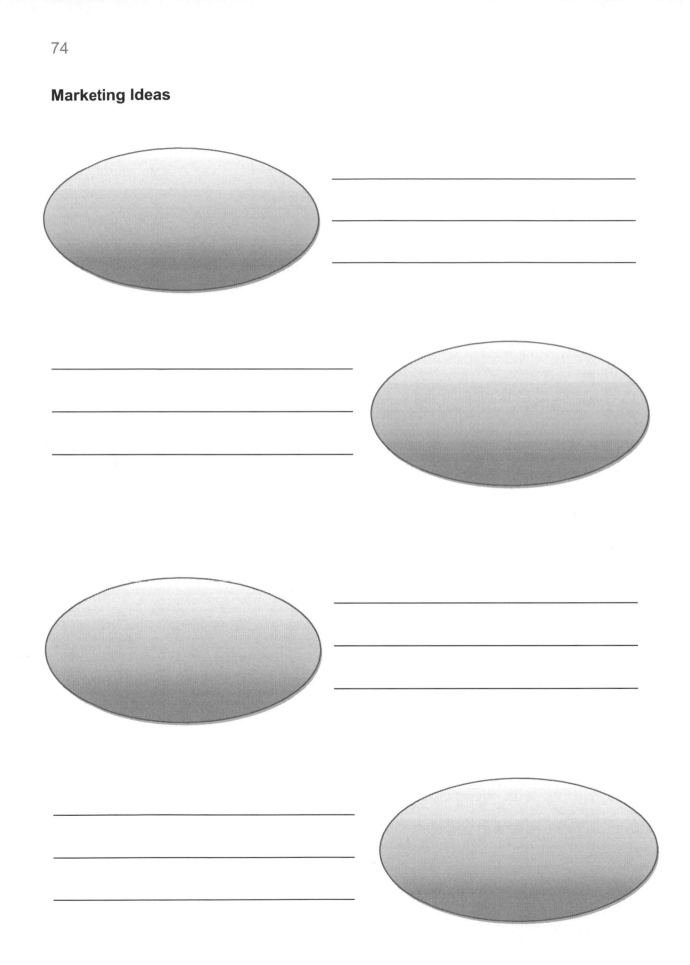

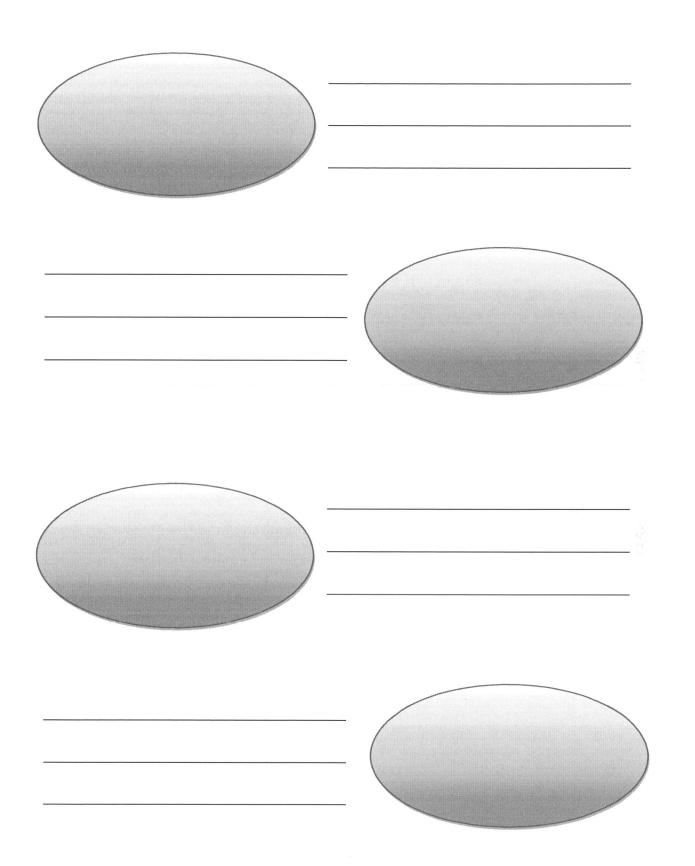

75

Writer´s Workbook

© Tanja Hanika, www.tanja-hanika.de

Marketing Plan

When?	What?	Where / Who?

Social Media Plan

Table to help you planning your social media activities.
Tip: Start your marketing before you publish the book to reach as many readers as possible.

Date	Facebook	Twitter	Instagram	YouTube	Blog	...	...	Link	Picture	Video	...	Title of the article

Schedule ☑

(Personal) Deadline	Task	

The Voice of the Author and the Author as a Brand

What do I want to stand for? What makes my stories special?

....
....
....
....
....

What is my area of expertise?

....
....

How do I want to be noticed as a brand?

....
....

What shall the plotted story stand for?

....
....
....
....
....

What is its USP (Unique Selling Proposition)?

....
....

How does the story fit my brand?

....
....
....

Copies for Review

Contacted Reviewer	Blog / Website / ...	Acceptance / Rejection	Target Date

Blog Tours

Blog Contacted	Answer?	Content	Date

Press Release

A press release informs journalists about upcoming publications.

Be careful: sometimes they are released word by word.

Do not forget the copyright when using author photographs or other pictures.

Structure of a press release:

- If available, use your logo

- Recipient´s address

- Sender´s address

- Mention "Press Release" as subject matter

- Date

(The press release text that you want published starts here!)

- Title

- Where appropriate, appealing subtitle or tagline

- Text (the "lead" in the first paragraph should contain the most important information)

(The press release text that you want to be published ends here!)

- Details about copyright

- Short biography

Final tips:

- Write short and objective sentences

- Answer journalistic "w-questions" (Who? What? When? Where? How? Why?)

- Mention an embargo period, if necessary, if you don't want the press release published
  before a certain date

What is the title?

What is the subtitle / tagline?

Draft of the article:

_____

_____

_____

_____

_____

_____

_____

_____

_____

_____

_____

_____

_____

_____

_____

_____

_____

_____

_____

List of required Copies

How many Books do I need for each purpose?

Bloggers: _____

Copies for (online) Book Groups: _____

Proof Copies (libraries, designers, etc.): _____

Own Sales: _____

Copies for the press: _____

Presents: _____

Further Marketing (Raffles, etc.):_____

Stock: _____

[   ]: _____

[   ]: _____

[   ]: _____

[   ]: _____

Total: _____

_____

_____

_____

_____

_____

_____

_____

_____

Synopsis

> When you are submitting to a publisher or an agency, the synopsis is one of the most important parts. Take care when writing it and make use of the following tips.

Checklist of what should be included:

[ ] Name, address and contact details

[ ] Working title

[ ] Is it written in the present tense?

[ ] Keep it short – no more than three A4 pages.

[ ] Break up paragraphs to make it easy to read.

[ ] Stick to the submission guidelines of the publisher/ agent.

[ ] Do not forget the covering letter!

Content:

[ ] Would a quotation at the beginning help sell your book?

[ ] How long is the novel (word count)?

[ ] What is the premise?

[ ] What is the genre?

[ ] Include only a small amount of background information

[ ] Who provides the narrative voice? From who's point of view is it told?

[ ] Synopsis (do not use cliffhangers and do not try to create tension with an open end!)

[ ] Include protagonists and important side characters; show their motivations, development and aims

[ ] Conflicts

[ ] Who is your target audience?

[ ] What is different / new about your novel? Why is it worth reading?

Checklist, what to avoid:

[ ] Do not use an invasive commercial style, no blurb

[ ] Do not re-narrate the whole novel, but carve out the central conflicts

[ ] Do not provide an interpretation of the text

[ ] Do not compare your book with other books or yourself with other authors

Notes for future Interviews

What do I want to emphasize about myself (Author as a Brand)?

....
....
....

What shall be emphasized about the Book Project?

....
....
....

What could be interesting about the writing process?

....
....
....

Is there anything interesting about the research?

....
....
....

What inspired me to write the book?

....
....
....

Which aims do I have regarding this book and my career?

....
....
....

[   ]?

....
....
....

Readings and Signings

Possible locations:

Practice reading aloud, perhaps record and analyze it. Be creative in marketing. Invite the press. Claim a fee! Bring a pen to sign books. Will you need change? Will you have to make out invoices? Be authentic, but original. Plan a talk in the end.

> _____   > _____

> _____   > _____

> _____   > _____

> _____   > _____

Ideas on how to turn the reading into an event:

[ ]

[ ]

[ ]

[ ]

[ ]

[ ]

[ ]

Concept A:

Concept B:

Concept C:

Possible passages to read aloud:

-
-
-
-
-

Program:

_____

_____

_____

_____

_____

_____

_____

_____

_____

_____

List of Contacts

List of important contacts. Include beta readers, bloggers, journalists, editors, designers, etc.

Name	Occupation	Contact Detail
A		
B		
C		
D		
E		
F		
G		
H		
I		

J		
`		
K		
L		
M		
N		
O		
P		
Q		
R		
S		

T		
U		
V		
W		
X		
Y		
Z		

Further notes:

_____

_____

_____

_____

_____

_____

_____

Notes

_____

_____

_____

_____

_____

_____

_____

_____

_____

_____

_____

_____

_____

_____

_____

_____

_____

_____

_____

_____

Glossary

Antagonist (p. 16, 17, 37, 38, 39, 68, 69, 70): The protagonist's opponent. The antagonist is the villain in the story. It can also be a kind of power, which sums up everything that opposes the hero on his way or delays him reaching his goals.

Atmosphere (p. 86): Setting and style of narration create a mood that underlines the plot of the story.

Background Story (p. 36, 37): A character's past. What did he/she experience, before he/she got into the story? Objects can have a background story as well.

Beginning (p. 40, 41, 43): The everyday life of the protagonist and/or of all the characters before the plot starts. It shows the state at the beginning of the story, before the hero starts his/her adventure and develops himself/herself.

Chapter Changeover (p. 50, 51, 68, 73): The last scene in a chapter cannot only end with a cliffhanger, but it should also hint at the next chapter or mark a clear ending. Good chapter endings can bond the reader to the story.

Characters (p. 5, 9, 15, 16, 17, 18 ff, 36, 53, 56, 64, 68, 69, 73, 86): The persons, who occur/act in the story.

Cliffhanger (p. 86): Exciting point at the end of a chapter, where the way out of a problem (solution) is not revealed yet.

Climax (p. 43, 52): The most important point regarding conflicts and tension. Here, the hero wins or loses. The course of the rest of the story is decided here.

Cliché (p. 68): A commonly known and many times used story detail or character trait. Mostly, clichés hit the core of what the author tries to say, but for readers they are boring, and the text loses its freshness.

Complications/Impediments (p. 13, 14, 43, 69, 70): Problems the protagonist has to face and that make it harder for him/her to reach his/her goals.

Conflict (p. 7, 13, 14, 18 ff, 39, 42, 44, 52, 68, 86): Problems the characters have to face throughout the story. What prevents the hero from reaching his aim? Mostly, the conflicts get worse before they are solved.

Consequences (p . 69, 70): Consistencies that unfold because of the protagonist's actions or the things he/she has not done.

 © Tanja Hanika, www.tanja-hanika.de

Copies for Review (p. 80, 85): Books you give to bloggers for free so that they can read it and write an assessment on their blogs and on social media. Do not forget to get their affirmation that they really want to read the book first.

Crisis (p. 52): Tragic climax in a story. The worst, that could happen came true, and the protagonist has to deal with it.

Depth (p. 68): Characters are deep when they seem to be living persons and have three-dimensional traits. The bad guy, for instance, is not only evil but may also be likable in a special way or demonstrate a relatable behaviour so the reader can understand why he fights for his aims.

Filler Words (p. 68): Words used colloquially a lot, but without a real function in written texts. But take care, because those words cannot be deleted in every context.

Hook (p. 42): Primitive state in a story, which gets changed significantly during the plotline. First clues are visible early to get the reader's attention.

Inner Conflicts (p. 14, 18 ff): A character's inner fights with himself/herself.

Key Moment (p. 36, 37): An event, often in a character's past, that impresses on his/her being personality and future. The key moment influences decisions during the story and maybe even the ending of it.

Leitmotif (p. 68): An issue that runs like a thread through the whole story and develops it.

Location (p. 46, 49): The place where the story takes place.

Love Interest (p. 16): The character whose heart the protagonist tries to win. Both fall in love after they have solved a few problems.

Main Desire (p. 18 ff): What is the greatest need and the most important aim for the protagonist? Why is he/she willing to take all risks and to face all conflicts?

Main Plot (p. 56): The main plot encompasses the most important plot strand in the story, in which the protagonist fights to reach his/her aim.

Marketing (p. 74, 76, 77, 85): Marketing sums up everything the author does to win possible clients. The maintenance of client contacts as well as all strategies to raise book sales are part of the marketing.

Midpoint (p. 40, 41, 42): The midpoint does not necessarily have the highest tension. Here, it is decided why and how the hero will fight until the end.

Open Questions (p. 52, 53, 68): To raise the tension, the author can play with the reader's knowledge. At which point shall he/she know or suspect which things?

Pace of Narration (p. 68): The more description there is in the passage, the slower is the pace of narration. In action scenes with nearly no description, the pace is extremely high.

Pitch (p. 6): Short abstract of the project. The plot, main characters, and basic concept are outlined.

Plot (p. 13, 42, 43, 50, 56, 57, 68, 73): Plot means the action and the progress in the story. More than one plot string is possible and usual.

Plot Turn (p. 40, 41, 42, 43, 69): A point in the story when the hero is ready to give everything to reach his/her aim. He/she faces all fears and overcomes all impediments.

Problems (p. 14, 41, 49): The hero only reaches his aim if he grows and develops himself because of the problems he is facing through the story.

Protagonist (p. 7, 12, 13, 14, 16, 17, 36, 38, 39, 42, 47, 49, 52, 68, 69, 70, 86): Main character/hero of the story.

Resolution (p. 12, 14, 42, 52, 53): The resolution is not only about how the most important questions get resolved, but also about how the protagonist overcomes the conflicts and impediments he has to face during the story.

Scene (p. 5, 47, 55): Scenes divide acts in a drama as well as chapters in a novel. They are small units with similar content or themes or connected plot segments.

Setting (p. 8, 9, 45, 49, 68, 68, 70): Place and time of the story.

Solution (p. 12, 14, 42, 44, 52): The conflicts get resolved at the end, which means that the protagonist makes his way through the story and reaches his/her aim.

Stereotypes (p. 68): Insignificant side characters often are stereotypes. These are basic models that are well known in the literary corpus, but which tend to bore readers.

Subplot (p. 56): A plot besides the main plot, which mostly underlines the topics and plot structures of the main plot.

 © Tanja Hanika, www.tanja-hanika.de

Target Audience (p. 68): Readers whose interests, living circumstances, social surroundings, educational degree, etc. are considered in the story, which is therefore extremely appealing to this special group of persons.

Tension Arc (p. 68): The tension level throughout the story changes. While low in the beginning, when the base case is explained, it rises towards the end. During the course of the story, many new questions appear. Mostly, they appear when the reader gets the answer to a former question. That`s how the tension rises. After the climax, when most questions are answered, it sinks again.

Twist (p. 68): A surprising turn in the story, which was not obvious but is comprehensible with hindsight.

Also available by Tanja Hanika:

The Fear Monger
(Horror novel)

Fear, blood, pain.

Chester Harris wants more. He writes horror fiction and is no longer satisfied with shocking his readers with lurid and ghastly tales. To solve his dilemma, he invites unsuspecting guests to an evening of unspeakable gruesomeness. They must play a game of life and death. To survive, they must go beyond all limits their own and all those conceived to be human. Fear, blood and pain are on Chester's menu and his gluttony for this grisly fare knows no bounds.

Be forewarned: This horror novel contains explicit descriptions of violence and horrid details that will repulse the reader.

Made in the USA
Middletown, DE
09 February 2023

24437818R00057